Judge's Citation for *The Adjacent Possible*

"Gorgeously spare, hypnotic, the poems in *The Adjacent Possible* are a meditation on an 'adjacent' possibility '[w]ithout I, without / you,' the insight that 'the joint of two not solids . . . is no joint at all.' The poems in this collection beckon to the relationship of all beings, examine the 'flurried noises' of language, the 'substrata' of consciousness that distinguishes seer and seen, the eye the 'gracejoint.' Following the arc of seasons, 'particulars' of landscape 'accrete,' imitate the 'brief echoes of / an objective real' as filtered through the gaze of 'one' who 'still looks out' on ones that 'sound' and 'speak.' The language is part play, part theory: winter with its 'edges fringed with wintersedge,' spring when 'Lilies wave by / lovely / lovely,' when 'the is larks / through utter night, skirrs / at the hum of dawn,' summer 'most bodied, / the most seeming.' This 'radiant' poetic force, as heralded in the epigraph from Édouard Glissant, animates the 'mind's infoldings,' 'ghosts of / patterns, wisps crossing / an interior eye,' reduces to glance the 'cloudlight [that] tinks / at the atomic.' In the narrative arc, summer leaves us in the tenuous moment when the 'I / come into iridescence' perceives its shift from one to 'we,' asks 'if we [can] conjure beyond / a useless symbolic, without / order / unalone, no one.' It interrogates how we 'scaffold the abstract / fortifying the angles' of existence. The question of spring—'What is an I if / alone?'—is recollected at the end, in late summer, but with intensity exacted over time: 'will you be / still by me, still possible?'"

—**Kathleen Hellen**, author of *Umberto's Night*

THE ADJACENT POSSIBLE

THE ADJACENT POSSIBLE

Julie Phillips Brown

GREEN WRITERS PRESS *Brattleboro, Vermont*

Printed in the United States

10 9 8 7 6 5 4 3 2

Green Writers Press is a Vermont-based publisher whose mission is to spread a message of hope and renewal through the words and images we publish. Throughout, we will adhere to our commitment to preserving and protecting the natural resources of the earth. To that end, a percentage of our proceeds will be donated to environmental activist groups. Green Writers Press gratefully acknowledges support from individual donors, friends, and readers to help support the environment and our publishing initiative.

GReen
writers
press

Giving Voice to Writers & Artists Who Will Make the World a Better Place
Green Writers Press | Brattleboro, Vermont
www.greenwriterspress.com

ISBN: 978-1-9505845-8-1

COVER ART: *Poncho de alambre* by Cecilia Vicuña, c. 1986, mixed media, stone, and copper wire.

BOOK DESIGN: Julie Phillips Brown

PRINTED ON RECYCLED PAPER BY BOOKMOBILE.
BASED IN MINNEAPOLIS, MINNESOTA, BOOKMOBILE BEGAN AS A DESIGN AND TYPESETTING PRODUCTION HOUSE IN 1982 AND STARTED OFFERING PRINT SERVICES IN 1996. BOOKMOBILE IS RUN ON 100% WIND- AND SOLAR-POWERED CLEAN ENERGY.

for Aiden, my son
& Linda, my mother

In the linking of spontaneous and
nonspontaneous processes, the universe
as a whole advances autocatalytically
into its adjacent possible

—Stuart Kauffman, *Investigations*

Nous avons déjà prononcé
la force poétique dont nous pensons
qu'elle rayonne en place du concept
absorbant d'unité: c'est l'opacité
du divers, qui anime la transparence
imaginée de la Relation[1]

—Édouard Glissant, *Poétique de la Relation*

1   SUBSTRATA

5   WINTER

29   SPRING

53   SUMMER

73   LATE SUMMER

86   NOTES

SUBSTRATA

Whole fields curved
to the sway of
if

unwritten as it is, indeterminate
interminate

Without hints without hue
white

without I, without
you

without

And yes to *is*, to *does*;

yes to *and*, or, alternatively, to *or*.

Yes to winterfruit and other nouns,
to adjectival, adverbial rondures
and these flurried noises
yes
voices' scrattle in the white
cacophony of if,
fully

luminous

WINTER

Morning   the field curves toward the river, edges fringed
with wintersedge   Wind grazes an undulation of white hills

Waves of grasses stand as antennae, cast wide

the prescient crackle   The cold air blazes on—

Freighters haze over
backs of hills   horns sounding
down through the valley.

The hills course   wake
with industry; mote and floss
upon a dazzled iris,
heron in the reeds.

Jetstreak streams   white rough across a canopy

of downed silt

                Snowdraft slows in untraceable directions, blooms

in pale opulence. On the banks   particulars accrete,
        make a white   Houses crowd the hills and pinebrush.

There is an exhaustion of stars, and firebright   leaves gray cumuli gray,
        swollen. Solidly. Only a blackbird
                                silhouette
                                darts through it here, here.

                                        There—

pricks an unsystematic filigree over the distance.

        An atmosphere vined
        thick with weather, banks laden
                with the white of it.

        Clouds hold their encodings,
        their cyclonic ignitions—

technae undertow

Some ones fold wings to their bodies, their fluttered keels
first to surface.
                        They duck. Alternate
                                        as they swim through
                or range over intermittent ice flats.

They feather, edges of white moving among other whites   a precise
                        pantomime, camouflage

        of everywhere else. Squad of reedy faces, bright eyes seethe
                from the mudbeds

                A white river of
                animate particulars
                flocks as the abstract

                        intent toward that
                                empirical real

Some ones roll over the water now. Their arms make
a line of herringbone angles. Each oar pierces
            the water, sweeps flustered mallards to either side.
One sits astride the stern, calls to each of the others
            how to move their limbs. Their bodies. How breathe.
How skim. This is how one moves a craft.

            Arms advance forward,
backward, however—together.

            Twist topography, miscellany of rain

One other stands on the blotted riverbank. Light snow forms   hints at
      falling, sifts loosely

            among the stones and wateredge.

                              Across the sunglare,
                  the sideswept surface spreading,

                                    one waves in passing.

As the sun slides slant, it moves more slowly.
Ones move more slowly. The river cuts deep into its bed.

Oars given over, the keels bump at the dock.
In the low-hung branchspread   leaves curl inward,

make a deckled umberwood.

Ochre and violet have the run of the hills.

Cloud passes cloud
        opaquely; the whole of white

drifts in gunmetal light.

Darkling, it makes a black. A crinkled slick. Thicked over,
unmoving. No one is by the river.

Lights twinkle from the window frames, houses all shut.
One still looks out to see   the movement that is not there,
                                 the quelled pitch   that is.

        Each one lies asleep
        in its own life, dreams   a lark

              keen incongruence

The willow branches at the riveredge lean toward daybreak,
buds coiled within fur sheaths. Tightly, a furled pressure.
Corms, tubers bursting
in earth   Initiate an aeration, siphon

the atmospheric expanse

ranging above.

From noplace, two ones—
an emergence in the white,
of the white, they cleave
a blind parallel

One scales a rising, back to the hills and climbing fullheight.
The rocks cast rocks upon rocks. One angles

against earthrise   flight skyward

One emerges, a small vertical at the riveredge. One watches, waves as.
By the bank, waking. Wan to the river's wake

one

One rifles over the prospect of scapular hills, scans a metered
distance   Breath and analogous cloud surface the mountain

One sounds the waters, breaks toward a bottom of delimitation.
Fathomless   remains the river, remains one   each at the last.

One turns the eye under cloudcover, an open pool—blue running
onto blue, lapsed distances   One blinks at haze of ice   snowfall

One furls the tongue at the riveredge, uncinctures the word
and the real. Cracked breath of language. One slips under,
                                        wonders   seeded dream.

A cloudself

One flowers among the watery veils   outpalm, open

One scatters unrelational, dearticulates toward an unthinking unthought
Spun pinions   mind of atmosphere

Under under. Unaccountable, one is countless, fathomless, and alone.
Words form as burrs and pits. The river, the mouth   weeps

One forms with a question   listens for precipitate ontologies
to enter the ear   curl in its cupola

One lingers in an uncompleted state, wonders toward an other one

Bodied echo of the real. An eye, a leaf, a crown

One strikes out toward the proposition. One traces over a wide
of snowfall. One in one's own drift, watching   One wakes as air

One is one, suffices.

20

If we   should speak,
                          should we
cancel ourselves or submit,
graze the edge of if

If not, the semblance of we
will echo blankly, repeat
will echo blankly.

As wave to a wave,
foreign song without human
meaning, human feeling

a gold-feathered bird
Our words undo themselves, soft—
listen—they break even as we

Each glance spun toward insensate
purpose   the harlequin space
between

Your voice echoes   rubied
snow over mountain ridge,
        flares out, exhausts
over near distances.

The mountain rushes back
down the throat like seadrift.

                                How does an unceasing I
                                fractionate itself, or
                                begin   as it ends,
                                snaked reverberation,
                                some lucid symmetry?

An eye runs the length
of the word, that image
of the mind: the you yourself,
and it is no picture at all.

Recall that dream of limits
undone or traversed,
the chance of one body
gesturing toward another,
the empathic inmost
other   open

The field ceases to tremble   Hushed tips of grasses, the way
landscape unmoves

Magnetisms break.

Only the trees
shaped as memory now   Grow blackly

in the pale.

Each one estranges itself, peels offward. As a we comes apart,
sparks intermittently in gloam and pith   Ones resolve

to the planetary,

drift toward dusk

toward equilibrium

A mere mere reports
from the world, brief echoes
of an objective real.

One runs in a region of endless mountains, proofs the absolute singular.

One thrills at windrush, and the curvature
of shoulder to limb to rockpeak   Run together
in a hunched range.

One ventures toward
the limits, stone and crevasse.
Flights of ice touch down.

The river revolves in its bed and cuts the field more deeply.
Its mouth opens out to an expanse, salts over.

One threshes
among shoots and fibrous matter,

loosens driftwood and grit from the bank. Roots atomize
in the marshloam

One plucks at cattails, weaves among the stalks.

A fossil sealake,
coiled shells bedded like ears
in silt and sandstone.

SPRING

Yellowgreen rivulets
begin in the white, manifest
reticulations, the bare
temporal of if

Clouds trundle and break in a pale gold light   Early lilac
                                       blooms on the branch.

    Bare buds lie pinched. Rainfall hangs   a second atmosphere

condenses, falls in a thresh

        of fat drops. The brittle pod cracks its mouth—

        Floating seed
    to senseless sky,

senseless.

Ones swim on the river now, chins skimming the surface.

One casts a head forward, and the body follows.
More ones follow.

On the bank, ones stream a long-necked line of ambles.
Some small ones test ancestral eyes and tendons,

remember without memory

What rude configurations of cells
cycle, what prosperous encodings.

One settles on
a swatch of newgreen clover,
nips and swallows.

One sits on a rock by the river, where one other lies still. One watches the scales flashing at the sun, flaking loose. One sloughs to atoms, waters and earthens its own stuff   Fans its ribs in a stretch

                              of sunglare.

    Lilies wave by,
    lovely,
    lovely.

The mountain warms and rises beyond the river, and the wind

rushes and rises. One glides on the current

                      open talons   flecked horizon.

    One feathers out

in mottled blue   broods on

                            an other one below

One cycles over in the mind, the unmoving revolutions. The eye
fixes on climbing muscle, stilted bone, degrees of vertical rise.

One toes at the shells, brings belly to water and sandbed. Salt waves
                  against rock   laps a shelf to hang from, launch

Flakes shudder in sidelong formations, settle widewise in a breathy field.
One leaps the static cracks. The crystals pack more densely.

One lies in the drift of a massive unspecific   undoes—

One imagines the body in space, all its apparent causality. One attempts
to affix the schema and the mountain looms   it is no landscape.

There is no horizon, no sail away toward

One sees only the joint

of two not solids, two not ones   it is no joint at all.

One imprints deliberately, casts an image of the other one,
smooth negative in snow.

One casts the mind toward a nonvisible   across the intersubjective,

the infinite horizons between

One remembers the other, the mind careening after
the already seen, the déjà   Deliriumdétente.

⊏⊐

Distance flickers with conception. Blood and muscle beat
an unseen beacon   One beckons across

Wind whips off white peaks, a whirr   One calls, an echo
reports   from the shrill rockface   Only one's one
One wonders toward response

The field runs low   one other is not here

What of that adjacent field—
lovers' synchronicities, cilia,
uncharted swarm minds, each
potent with the possible.
How we want for it, and why

We listen, intent
toward the objective,
that fragile if—

In turbulence, floes
drift, each inconsistency
foundering in the twilight
of the real.

Is the causal the singular
concern? What contingencies
still uncover the actual, the is
of things?   Or perhaps mere
looking, lids tendered to land-
scape, casts all in relief

We scaffold the abstract,
fortifying the angles
of untrue coalescences.

No—the is larks
through utter night, skirrs
at the hum of dawn

Then we draw mere slant
constellations in the offing,
course a chance current; if we
run bare against the real,
it is no magnificence.

The floor falls away, walls
break open in windows;
limitless, we molt
the singular

Flicker   trace a circuit
that is meaning as it happens,
means because it happens.

A casual causality, a seeming
netted glimmer

We might entangle ourselves,
thorny limbs, opaque

We assemble, bound
in tenuous semblance.
The possible ignites an I
in wonder, the temporary
belief   You are not
unlike me. Mere
articulate automata—
is this a we?

No, there is
some unspeakable charm
emerges, you or I;
insofar as we form a question,
an inclination. It is
an actual charm. It is.

One searches the spark,
internalizes, and a charm
disintegrates.

One accounts for
        thresholds between,
mechanical determinacies.

Then an I might turn
to the mind's infoldings
where you are not
with me.

What breaks the absolute singular,
breaks it all   breaks at all
breaks all

What is an I if
alone   a lone   all
one   all

Our thoughts   trued
synchrony   course on
tremulous gold of spirules
waves in a field.

The mountains break
across the sky

If we conjure beyond
a blank symbolic, without
order   unalone
what then, whither

Ones strike toward divergent fields.

River and no mountain, or else mountain and no river.

        Each courses   consistent within
   its own constraints   Imagines a self
                        self-defined
                              sufficient

Each staggers without
co-implication   the inner
lists   an abstract

The river ebbs, sinks closer to earth and away. Runs offward
to snatch at horizons   tendered by limits

Restless, the river hums
between its banks and mudbed.

The mountain recedes from the riverplain   practices
height and prospects

of distance.

Its peaks range over rivers, slate streams in the sky   Air runs
as a gulf, a watery eye scattered, softly prismatic

Clouds form, heave under
a haze of unforms,
and one.

SUMMER

A green green thickly
emergent, the fully fragrant
leaves before a fall.

Each one a deep green
steeped in successive waves
of light   Ones rumble,
burst above equilibrium. It is
the most bodied,
the most seeming.

Azure settles on a fragrant green   the sun, fully   A swarm of ones
                    paddle across the river. Shuttle and swipe.

        In the shallows, ones puff and nip

        Claws clink on the rocks.

                Each small intelligence
                        scuttles loose, makes a minute
                            dire real.

Two ones recline on a lip of grasses
                          by the bank,
                              a sometime sealake. One angles
          an elbow, watches
                    where an other lies sleeping   Sunglint on

                              a fan of gold hair.

            The ridges of waves run on   Chipped peaks
                                                    hills.

                              One grazes the skin
                              of the other   Fingertips
                                    flecked irises

The river lies lowly   Waters return to the atomic,

                                                    clamber and scale

The mountainface   rises as cloudfields.

            River gathers as dark,
        a sky dense with embers

The mountain streams toward riverplain, shakes loose a frigid gale—

        The air rolls downward
    in boulders, edged

rough as thunder.

The rockface ratchets across the cracking.

⊏⊐

Cold lunges on warm air   Sound and light shatter in jags
over the river. The sky lows at the surface. One runs, whipped by wind.

The rocks tumble down the face and one scurries   Bursts brightly
in the brain, the strumming constellation of a hive mind.

One glimpses, lists after as   One other streaks, a blotted ghost,
and the river pours from the sky.

One lies on the mountainface, on earth run wet

A canopy of leaves bends earthward. Branches cleave a field

                        in two   One scarcely

One tumbles with the rockface toward the river.

Indigo sky spattered bright

A softened plain. A single field, entire   Fled, wet.

One thunders faintly   The water recedes with the riverbed, nightfall.

Flutters an eye. Skin memory, the not possible

                        Touch in an umbermind

One rushes where one lies still   cracks wide in a vibrant daze

Across a blackly blaze, ones mark a joint of eye, the barest gaze.

Your dream of the present—
worlds counted, each particular
precisely particular   All that is
solid, shed

Let us be unspeakable,
unemergent, unrealized—
some possible, un in fact.

Phantom patterns
cross an interior eye

recollected, the self
appeals to mere intuition,
an insinuation of insight.

Is it the inmost inner,
darkest, gritted glass
by which we see?
Does it show slanted
the true

        Or is it no gleam
at all—the actual self
burned across the atmosphere
of its own external limits

An actuality in the gloam,
an I comes to iridesence,
shatters unsaid innumerables.
Unaccountable, infinite arches
branching a blank sky.

Light lowers, unbound   We try
the particulars   The possible
leaps its blank dance
        a distant arc
we know by touch

The iridesence is here
It is   latent, lambent.

This unsteady dialogue
convolves. We wait, each
word halting on lip, tooth;
we speak in tongues
unfamiliar, lose all
insight   sea

We speak   an open field   wakes
            the natural dissonance
of relation arises, the way
a body articulates
in wordless exchange

LATE SUMMER

The field trembles with voices   Floss, white noises carried on breeze

Each voice echoes after

its other, reticulates notches,

touches down in air

The river wanders, the mountain wanders. Ones perturb a single field,
its saturate media. Ones ring with turbulence

as eye slides

over eye,

a glancejoint

Leaves dew, curl closed against nightfall. The air sinks warmly over
grasses by the river.

Ones speckle the twilight, a glitter craze.

Has it been always
an entire field, the same

field

have we always

Ones dally in a white light, blushed under the skin. Ones trace
     an unfamiliar chitter

          of eye, shoulder   Ones drift, laze

     in a subjunctive mode

One autocatalyzes, sparks with a charm, and lights

for its immediate other to see

Its other answers an echo

                                 lights

More others now

        A whole field of lights

        sways across

river inlet, rises

        toward peaking mountains

A late cloudlight tinks
at the atomic

Fly, fire

Imagine the beautifully adjacent—
as arms, as echoed hearts,
the perturbed possible
that fires the skin, pierces
the eye. The palm at the end
of each mind, that which delimits,
blazes brightly, and means
because it is.

That star-eyed if   As each of us forms
with the question

will you be
still by me, still possible?

ACKNOWLEDGEMENTS

I am deeply grateful to Kathleen Hellen for selecting this manuscript for the 2019 Hopper Poetry Prize, and to Dede Cummings, Rachel Nolan, and Green Writers Press for shepherding this book into being. My thanks to the editors of *Denver Quarterly*, *Peregrine*, and *Posit*, for first believing in these poems.

Many of the passages in *The Adjacent Possible* reflect the years of rich conversations I enjoyed with Benjamin Alexander Logsdon, as well as the keen and generous readerships of Alice Fulton, Roger Gilbert, and Kenneth McClane. My deepest thanks to Dana Koster, for her forebearance and companionship through many long Ithaca winters and springs, as we wrote our first manuscripts side by side. My gratitude to Gabrielle Calvocoressi, who showed me the way toward these poems in their final forms, and to Robert Hass, whose attention to these poems at Sewanee was a gift.

I cannot think what my life would have meant without the mentorship of Gregory Djanikian and Susan Stewart, each of whom taught me what it was to be a poet, and how it might be possible. Thank you. And thank you to my writing partner and dear friend, Deborah Miranda. Your presence is a cherished gift, now and always.

Most of all, I am grateful to my family for their ceaseless support, which is a debt I can never repay. To David and Aiden, who have taught me fathomless love: thank you with all of my heart.

NOTES

[1] In English translation, the epigraph from Édouard Glissant reads, "We have already articulated the poetic force. We see it as radiant—replacing the absorbing concept of unity; it is the opacity of the diverse animating the imagined transparency of Relation."

—*Poetics of Relation*, translated by Betsy Wing